STORY : **ARNAUD DELALAND**
DRAWING : **LAURENT BIDO**
COLORING : **CLÉMENCE JOLL**

WITH **JOSEPH WEISMANN**
TRANSLATED BY **RICHARD KUTNER**

AFTER the ROUNDUP

ACKNOWLEDGMENTS

Our heartfelt thanks go to Joseph Weismann for trusting us and standing by us throughout the deeply moving experience of creating this book.

We would like to express our gratitude as well to his granddaughter Iris, the first to hear about this project and to tell Joseph about the authors' idea of adapting his life to the graphic novel format.

We are grateful to his son, Francis, thanks to whom this project has come to fruition. Francis's initiative in approaching the publisher Michel Lafon allowed us to use *Après la Rafle*, written by Joseph in collaboration with Caroline Andrieu, as a reference.

Thanks also go to Joseph's daughter Isabelle for her support.

We thank Nicole Zlatiev-Scocard for her careful rereading and insightful suggestions.

Finally, we would like to express our gratitude to Bertille Comar, Laurent Muller, and the publisher Les Arènes for supervising the production of this book.

Preface

I was born in Paris in 1931. In 1942, I was eleven years old, and I wore the yellow star.

My parents, my two sisters, and I were arrested on July 16, 1942, during the big Vél' d'Hiv' Roundup, before being taken to the Vélodrome d'Hiver cycling stadium. We stayed there five days and five nights, without food, water, or sanitation. Then we were transferred to the internment camp of Beaune-la-Rolande, in the Loiret region of France. After being held for about two weeks, the rest of my family was sent to the Auschwitz extermination camp, in Poland. As soon as they arrived, they were gassed and burned in the crematory ovens.

Even with the gendarmes, watchtowers, and barbed wire, I managed to escape from Beaune-la-Rolande with my friend Joe, who was as bold as I was.

Despite the collaboration of the Vichy government, the entire French population cannot be considered guilty. Of all the occupied countries, France had the smallest percentage of French and foreign Jews sent to the camps. We should also remember that 75 percent of the Jews of France survived. In 1995, President Jacques Chirac finally acknowledged the participation of the French state in the fate of its Jews: the government had indeed abandoned to the occupier a segment of its population that it should have protected. This admission was an immense comfort to me.

Urged on by Simone Veil well before this, I began to reflect on an obligation that was mine as well after such a long silence: the duty to bear witness, the necessity to be willing to tell others about what I had lived through. For more than forty years, I have visited countless middle and high schools in France and abroad, a commitment that led to my being named Officier de la Légion d'Honneur and to my receiving the Palmes Académiques (for distinguished contributions to education). In Le Mans, where I have lived for decades, the Villaret Middle School became the Joseph Weismann Middle School in 2019, a source of great pride for me.

The narrative that you are about to discover inspired Rose Bosch's film *La Rafle* (*The Roundup*), which was released in 2010. It was essential, though, to tell the rest of the story: in collaboration with Caroline Andrieu and the publisher Michel Lafon, I wrote the memoir *After the Roundup*, which came out in 2011. Then a lucky coincidence put me in contact with the artist Laurent Bidot, who, along with the author and scriptwriter Arnaud Delalande, created the graphic novel that you have in your hands. After the film and the book, it was of the greatest importance that it be realized.

This book has a specific goal: the unceasing transmission, to the young as well as the old, of the memory of one of the darkest pages of the history of humanity, the Holocaust ("Shoah" in Hebrew, meaning "catastrophe"), a word that designates the murder of nearly six million European Jews by Nazi Germany and its collaborators.

I am one of its last survivors.

By means of this testimony, I wish to continue to inform people so that this tragedy never occurs again.

For my entire life, I have borne the terrible pain caused by the loss of my loved ones. But I have also developed a determination and an optimism that have succeeded in bringing down mountains, no doubt molding myself into an "example of psychological resilience," as the psychiatrist Boris Cyrulnik would say.

I am now ninety years old.

But I can still convey one last message: never accept the unacceptable.

JOSEPH WEISMANN
Le Mans, October 7, 2021

7

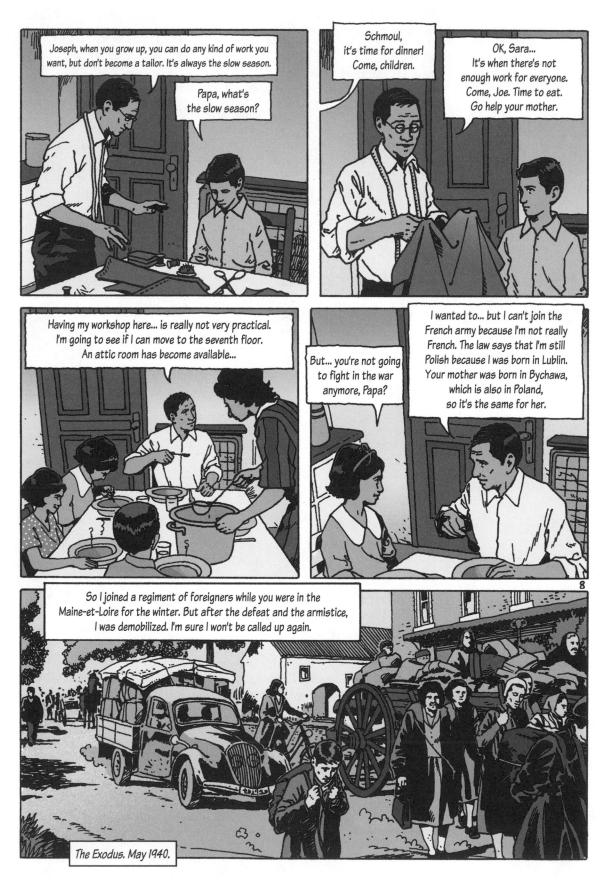

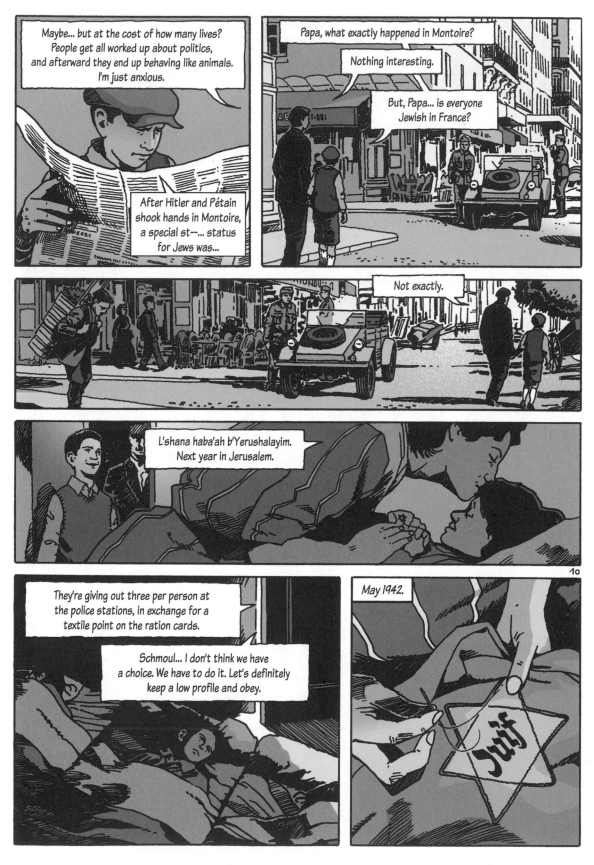

11

Thank you, gentlemen. I think that would satisfy my government. In that case, the agreement can be ratified as soon as possible. Nevertheless, there are many practical details to work out.

July 4, 1942. Paris, headquarters of the Gestapo.

Meeting between René Bousquet and Louis Darquier de Pellepoix, Commissioner-General for Jewish Affairs; SS Colonel Helmut Knochen; and SS Captain Theodor Dannecker, German chief of police in France.

We have a date. The roundup will take place on July 13, if that's all right with you.

We'll set up another meeting in Herr Dannecker's office, on Avenue Foch, to talk about how things will be organized.

I'll invite my second-in-command. We'll also need Jean François, head of the state police; Émile Hennequin, chief of the Paris police; Tulard, who's in charge of "Jewish affairs" at the prefecture... Garnier, for supplies...

... Ah! Also Guidot, the police captain... and finally Schweblin, Chief of Police for Jewish Affairs in the Occupied Zone. We're going to mobilize the government agencies!

Confiserie

AFFICHE OBLIGATOIRE
Jüdisches Geschaeft
ENTREPRISE JUIVE

15

Meeting on July 7, Avenue Foch.

So everyone's agreed? All the French police will have to do is carry out orders! The only thing that remains is to write up the memo...

Police Headquarters Memo n° 173–42 of 13 July 1942, ordering the roundup and arrest of 27,427 foreign Jews residing in France.

Police headquarters, July 13.

Hennequin signed it! It includes all German, Austrian, Polish, Czech, Russian, and stateless Jewish men ages 16 to 60, women 16 to 55, and their children.

Their children? Even those born in France?

Yes. Eichmann wants to reach the goal of 22,000, and Laval says he doesn't want to break up families. There are a few exceptions, but those are the orders. To avoid wasting time, we'll sort them at their first detention center rather than in their homes.

Print it in very large numbers... Roll the presses!

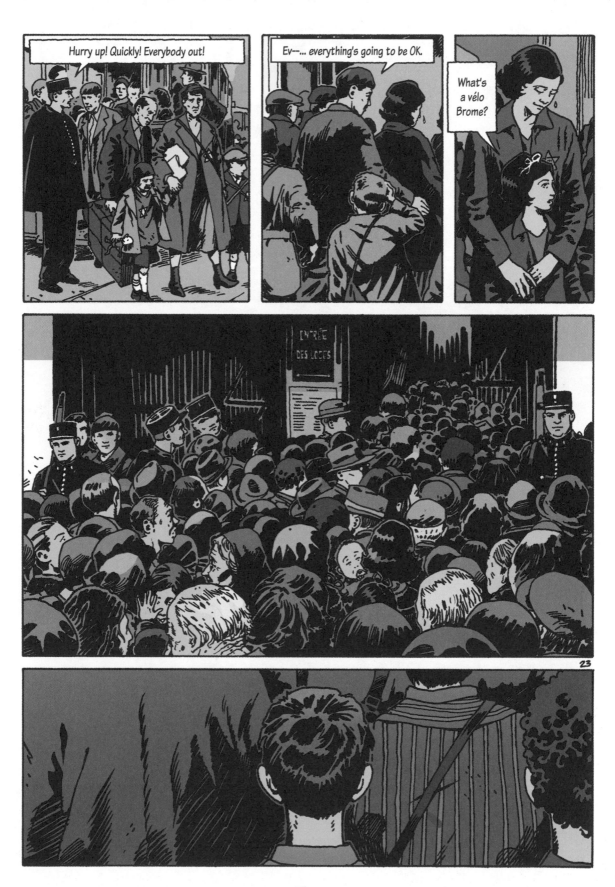

Gare d'Austerlitz (Austerlitz railroad station, Paris).

32

35

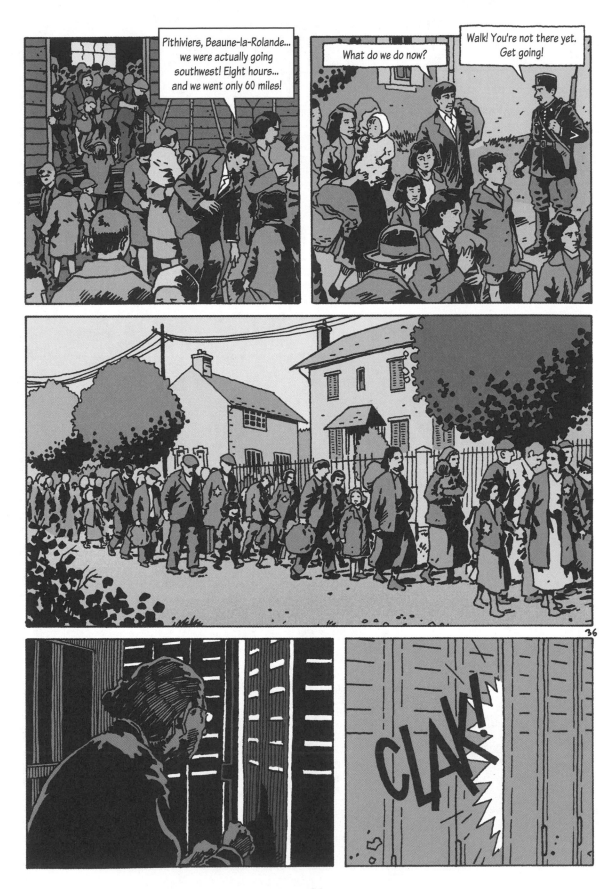

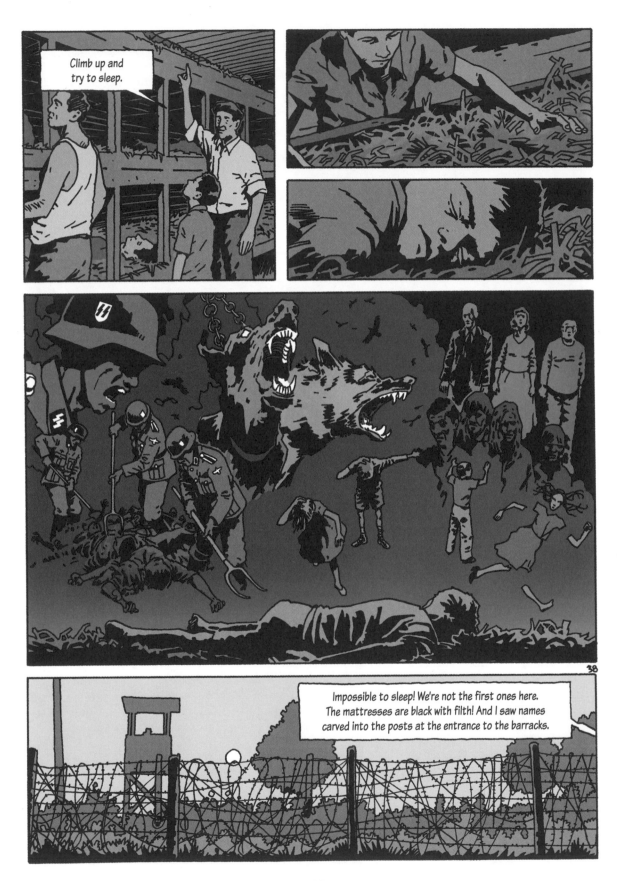

Climb up and try to sleep.

Impossible to sleep! We're not the first ones here. The mattresses are black with filth! And I saw names carved into the posts at the entrance to the barracks.

38

45

*Is everything going according to plan?

48

Pitchi Poi... Pitchi Poi...
We'll meet again in Pitchi Poi...

WHEYYEEEH!!

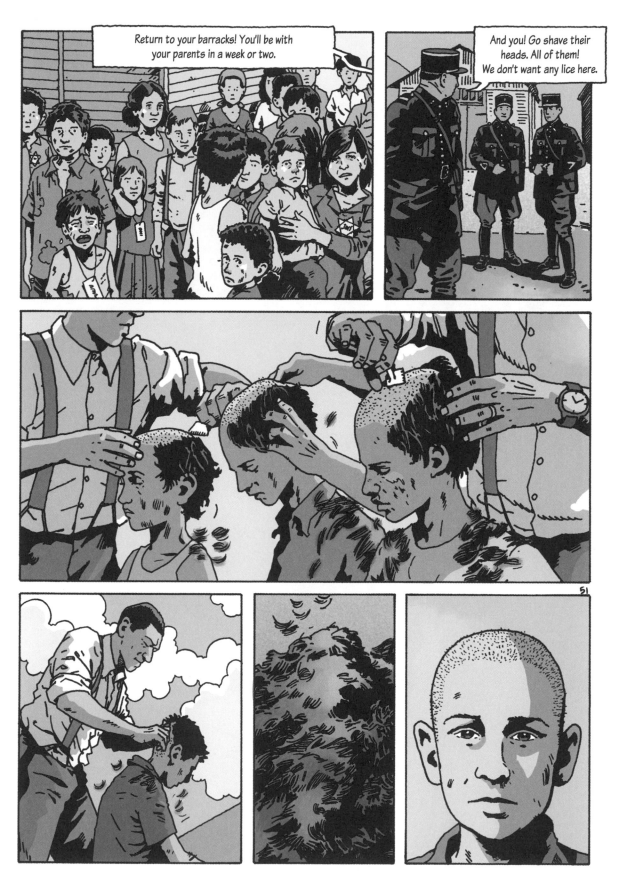

54

An escape plan, that's what I need. Getting out of here is easy to say... but doing it is another story. There are watchtowers, soldiers everywhere, and... all that barbed wire. It's at least 15 yards wide...

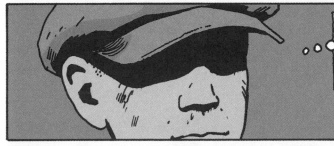

And I'll never be able to do it alone. At 55 pounds, I don't weigh much more than a German shepherd! I need to find someone... preferably someone strong!

But who'll dare? Who'll want to go with me?

Are you nuts? They'll shoot you like a rabbit!

Why do you want to leave? They said we'd be seeing our parents again in a week!

And you, Henri?

I-I'd like to... but I can't. I have a hernia.

*Joseph's real last name, changed to "Kogan" by his father to hide the family's Jewish roots.

DING!
DING!
DING!

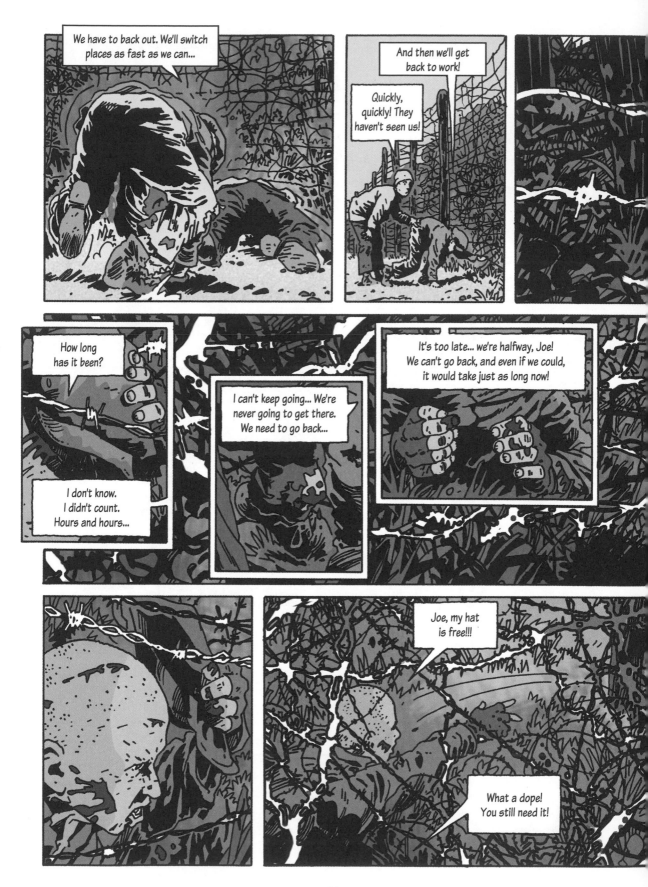

Hotel in New York, 1965.

JOE!!!

JOE!!!

72

Boys, I understand your situation. Listen to me carefully: Go to sleep now. Get some rest. Tomorrow you'll find the door open. There's a bus for Montargis. From there, you'll be able to take a train to Paris.

We never saw you.

There are at least two nice ones!

76

It's open!!

79

I sought refuge at Père Fabri's, in the café on Rue Cauchois. But the guest register of his little hotel was checked every day. So he placed me with a woman on Rue Saint-Rustique. Then I ended up at the orphanage in Rue Lamarck.

But... you were in Beaune-la-Rolande, too? What's your name?

André Schwarz-Bart. They let me out because I had tuberculosis. What about you?

Um... I escaped!

Ah, the hero!! So it was you, with your friend? Don't expect me to thank you! They were furious! If you only knew how miserable they made us afterward! They never stopped counting us... and there were so many of us that they always lost count!

But... the others? What about all the others?

I don't know.

The Germans came from time to time, and they always left with a few of us... They had to keep filling their record books...

I was sent to live with a foster family.

An elegant lady, whose husband was a lawyer. They had a magnificent apartment... I liked her right away! Suddenly, I had a real bedroom just for me, with a double bed!

But the problem was the grandmother, the lawyer's mother.

Ah! Joseph. Grandmother would like to speak with you.

Joseph, you took one of my rusks!

What? No, Madame, I swear! I would never...

I know it's true because I counted them. Admit that you stole it!

There was a terrible scene... The old witch just wanted an excuse to get rid of me. And she succeeded!

Thanks to the General Association of French Jews, I was placed with a railroad worker. He thought the "little Jew" coveted his apples... Then I went to Rue de la Pompe with two other children... then to the country. And each time, I returned to Rue Lamarck.

Joseph, what am I going to do with you?

OK... I'm sending you to the Rothschild Foundation orphanage. It's bigger, and you'll be safer there.

You'll see. It's like a city within a city. It has a school, dormitories, kitchens, even a synagogue.

We were placed in the Castle of Méhoncourt, near Le Mans, with dozens of other children. It had been occupied by the Germans and was still defiled by swastikas.

We stayed there for months. I was still a hero because of my escape. I got the nickname Imp there.

But we had to learn trades in preparation for what would come afterward. First, I was a tool and die maker; then I began to learn about carpentry. I really liked wood.

The castle was run by the OSE, the Children's Aid Society, which looked after Jewish children.

DING! DING!

From time to time, we'd hear a bell, and one of us would leave to live in a foster family.

Judith and Léa were finally reconnected with an aunt who worked in a circus in Paris. I was so happy for them...

As for me, I didn't consider myself an orphan... rather as someone who was being put up temporarily.

Hey! Americans! Americans!

I wasn't ready to live without my family. I wasn't ready for anything...

94

96

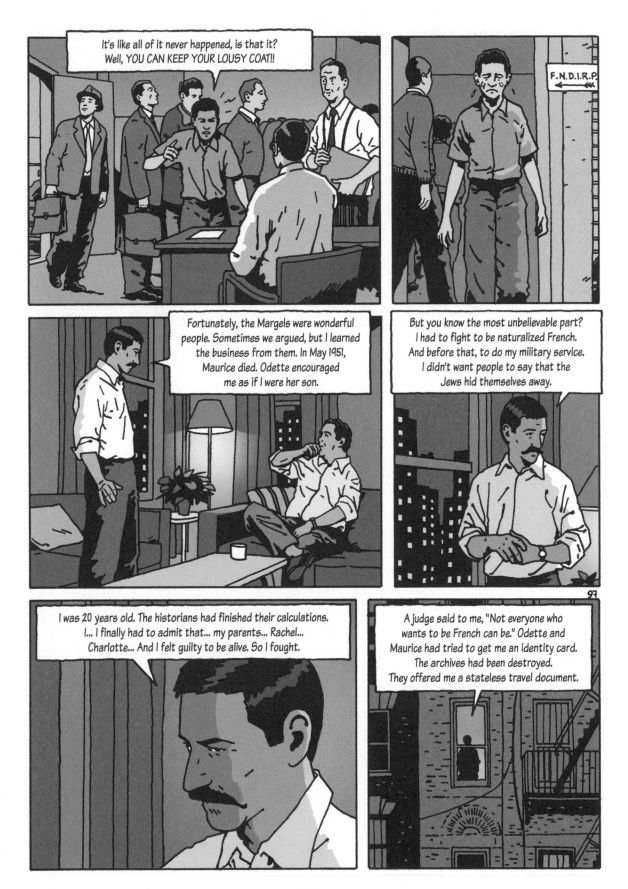

Have children. Be able to hold them by the hand, buy them beautiful schoolbags. Watch them grow. Grow old myself, watching them become adults. Love them like crazy.

I had a good client who ran a hotel-restaurant in a village near Le Mans. I would deliver bedding to her.

Joseph, come in and have a cup of coffee. My sister just arrived from England. You know she married an Englishman! She's here with her daughter. Come, I'll introduce her to you!

Her name was Francine. She was 25 years old and Jewish, like me... But she seemed to be a little ashamed of it.

We got married fairly quickly, at the French embassy, and we spent our honeymoon in a hotel run by a stingy woman in Brighton.

Look... we had three children: Francis, Nicole, and Isabelle.

They're beautiful!

99

Then the Lévitan furniture company asked me to represent them. They wanted to expand in western France. I accepted their generous offer but kept my independence. And... here I am!

Joe, we spent the whole night talking, and there's still so much to say. I still have a thousand questions to ask you.

Joseph, do you remember when you threw your hat through the barbed wire in Beaune-la-Rolande? We weren't free yet, though. Boy, was I mad at you then!

But you also made me laugh... and I've never stopped thinking about it. You know what we need to do now?

Now that we've been reunited... I have to go to France with my wife and daughter.

D950
BEAUNE-
LA-ROLANDE

100

Joe... Joe Kogan, you know... we could repeat this journey a thousand times, tear up our scalps on the rolls of barbed wire, sleep in the woods, knock on doors that no one opens...

We'll never really find peace...

...because we'll never ever stop wondering why all this happened.

I'm leaving New York for Las Vegas. The climate is better there. You know I have a weak heart.

We'll call and write to each other, right? For better or worse?

For better or worse.

4,115 children were dumped in the Vél' d'Hiv' and then interned here. The villagers saw them pass by their windows the first time, then again in the opposite direction when they were led to the railroad station for trains of no return.

And now?

Auschwitz, 1965.

107

CHODZENIE PO RUINACH
JEST NIEBEZPIECZNE

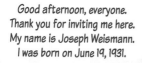

Good afternoon, everyone. Thank you for inviting me here. My name is Joseph Weismann. I was born on June 19, 1931.

I'm a citizen of France. But I don't belong to any race, neither a superior one nor an inferior one. I'm a member of the human race.

I was rounded up on July 16, 1942. My parents and my two sisters were gassed as soon as they arrived at Auschwitz and burned in the crematory ovens.

I was like you. Well, not really. I wasn't a teenager yet. I was a child, a street kid from Montmartre. And my whole life I've carried around... this burden, this emptiness inside me, this hole in my being. This aberration.

But you need to understand that I always wanted to find my place in French society. In 1974, my wife and children and I decided to try living on a kibbutz in Israel, which was still a nation under construction.

I had discovered that an old aunt lived there, and I had gone there once before. But it didn't work out.

And there, just before the discussion, I met a woman. She had joined the Resistance at age 16 and was sent to Auschwitz with her family.

She had arrived there late in 1944 and had escaped the gas chambers by lying about her age and being declared fit to work.

That woman was Simone Veil.*

She leaned toward me and, looking straight into my eyes with her clear, penetrating gaze, murmured to me...

You often tell your story to others, don't you?

*A French (Jewish) magistrate and politician who would become the first female president of the European Parliament.

No, not really. Why?

Monsieur Weismann, you must. You have a duty to bear witness.

So I began to speak. At first, I told my story to Blanche Finger and William Karel, who were putting together a book in the 1990s... I went on TV...

And since then, I-I've also been speaking in French middle schools and high schools. I try to make the students hear the voices of memory.

I take part in lectures, conferences, debates. I try to respond to your teachers' invitations.

In 1995, something very... important for all of us happened.

July 16, 1995.
Square of the Martyrs of the Vél' d'Hiv'.

Yes, the criminal madness of the occupier was assisted by some French people, by the French government.

France--land of the Enlightenment and of human rights, land of hospitality and asylum--France, on that day, committed an irreparable act. It failed to keep its word and delivered those under its protection to their executioners.

In Paris and in the provinces, 74 trains would depart for Auschwitz. 76,000 Jews deported from France would never return. Our debt to them cannot be erased.

In this matter, nothing is insignificant, nothing is commonplace, nothing is separable. Racist crimes, the defense of revisionist ideas, and provocations of all kinds--little comments and quips--are all drawn from the same source.

By not concealing the dark hours of our history, we are simply defending the idea of humanity, of human liberty and dignity.

With these words, President Jacques Chirac acknowledged France's responsibility in the Vél' d'Hiv' Roundup.
I was in Le Mans when I heard this speech. And I was overcome by a very powerful emotion.

We, the survivors of the Vél' d'Hiv', had been waiting for this moment for years.

This acknowledgment returned honor and dignity to the Jews of France.

In 2009, we made the film *The Roundup*,* in Hungary, in part inspired by my story. You probably know that the Vélodrome d'Hiver was demolished in 1959, like so many other symbols of Vichy.

The director, Rose Bosch, and her team had found a cycling stadium in Hungary that was almost identical. I went there with my family, as an adviser.

*La Rafle

But suddenly...

PAPA?! PAPA?! What's wrong?

I-I don't know... I don't feel good... Let's get out of here! This noise... It's suffocating in here... And the stench! It's horrible! Can you smell it?

But, Papa... there's no smell at all!

It was an... olfactory memory. Everything was coming back to me, even the smells. But in 1942, we weren't shooting a film... It was absolute, raw reality.

So that... that was the war for me. That of an eleven-year-old child, abandoned with other children in a camp full of orphans. Children lost in an adults' war who were trying to survive, surrounded by soldiers in collusion with a regime of hate.

Then... the life of an escapee, and of exile from myself. But I finally managed... to survive. For my loved ones.

My dear Joe... he died a few years ago.

He had a beautiful family. He probably lived as well as he could, after what happened to us. He was victorious. I still love him, of course. For better or worse.

Think about the victims, the dead, the survivors who struggled so that the memory of the Holocaust would live on. This is the most beautiful homage that we can offer them. And while we must remember, of course, we must also think about the future.

And so, in closing, I have only one more thing to say to you.

My name is Joe Weismann. And I beg you, my children...

Editorial Director: Laurent Muller

Editorial Assistant: Bertille Comar

Graphic Design: Éric Pillault and Jean-Philippe Meier

Photoengraving: Image Press Édition

Production: Louise Clément

Copy Editors: Laure Picard-Philippon and Isabelle Paccalet

ISBN: 979-10-375-0569-9

FOR INDIANA UNIVERSITY PRESS

Lesley Bolton, Project Manager/Editor

Tony Brewer, Artist and Book Designer

Brian Carroll, Rights Manager

Dan Crissman, Trade and Regional Acquisitions Editor

Samantha Heffner, Trade Acquisitions Assistant

Brenna Hosman, Production Coordinator

Katie Huggins, Production Manager

Dan Pyle, Online Publishing Manager

Stephen Williams, Marketing Manager

Jennifer Witzke, Senior Artist and Book Designer

This book is a publication of

Indiana University Press
Office of Scholarly Publishing
Herman B Wells Library 350
1320 East 10th Street
Bloomington, Indiana 47405 USA

iupress.org

Adapted from *After the Roundup: Escape and Survival in Hitler's France* © Joseph Weismann, 2017, translated by Richard Kutner

Manufactured in the United States of America

First printing 2023

Cataloging information is available from the Library of Congress.

ISBN 978-0-253-06648-0 (paperback)

JOSEPH WEISMANN is a survivor of the 1942 Vél' d'Hiv' Roundup in Paris. Until he was 80, Weismann kept his experiences to himself, giving only the slightest hints of them to his wife and three children. Simone Veil, lawyer, politician, president of the European Parliament, and member of the Constitutional Council of France, urged him to tell his story. It would inspire the French film *La Rafle*. Now 92 years old, Joseph lives in Le Mans.

RICHARD KUTNER is an independent literary translator. His translations include *Fear of Paradise* by Vincent Engel and *Cast Away on the Letter A* by Fred, for which he was awarded a Hemingway Translation Grant by the Book Department of the French Embassy in the United States.